Contents

Unit 1   Letter B 4
Phonemic Awareness: Listening for the /b/ Sound; Listening for Rhyming Words
Vocabulary: Following Oral Directions
Comprehension: Categorizing
Visual Discrimination: Seeing the Whole
Fine Motor Skills: Using Scissors; Tracing

Unit 2   Letter R 10
Phonemic Awareness: Listening for the /r/ Sound
Vocabulary: Following Oral Directions
Comprehension: Predicting
Visual Discrimination: Seeing the Whole; Recognizing Objects by Shape
Fine Motor Skills: Using Scissors; Tracing

Unit 3   Letter F 16
Phonemic Awareness: Listening for the /f/ Sound; Listening for Rhyming Words
Vocabulary: Following Oral Directions
Comprehension: Categorizing
Visual Discrimination: Seeing the Whole; Identifying Likenesses and Differences
Fine Motor Skills: Using Scissors; Tracing

Unit 4   Letter C 22
Phonemic Awareness: Listening for the /c/ Sound
Vocabulary: Following Oral Directions
Comprehension: Sequencing Events
Visual Discrimination: Seeing the Whole; Identifying Missing Parts
Fine Motor Skills: Using Scissors; Drawing; Tracing; Tracking Left to Right

Review B, R, F, C 28
Phonemic Awareness: Listening for Sounds of /b/, /r/, /f/, /c/
Vocabulary: Following Oral Directions
Fine Motor Skills: Tracing

Unit 5   Letter M 30
Phonemic Awareness: Listening for the /m/ Sound
Vocabulary: Following Oral Directions
Comprehension: Predicting
Visual Discrimination: Seeing the Whole; Identifying Missing Parts
Fine Motor Skills: Using Scissors; Drawing; Tracing

Unit 6   Letter L 36
Phonemic Awareness: Listening for the /l/ Sound
Vocabulary: Following Oral Directions
Comprehension: Categorizing
Visual Discrimination: Seeing the Whole; Identifying Likenesses and Differences
Fine Motor Skills: Using Scissors; Tracing

Unit 7   Letter G 42
Phonemic Awareness: Listening for the /g/ Sound; Listening for Rhyming Words
Vocabulary: Following Oral Directions
Comprehension: Sequencing
Visual Discrimination: Seeing the Whole
Fine Motor Skills: Tracing; Using Scissors

Unit 8   Letter H 46
Phonemic Awareness: Listening for the /h/ Sound
Vocabulary: Following Oral Directions
Comprehension: Categorizing; Predicting
Visual Discrimination: Seeing the Whole; Identifying Likenesses and Differences
Fine Motor Skills: Using Scissors; Tracing

Review M, L, G, H 52
Phonemic Awareness: Listening for Sounds of /m/, /l/, /g/, /h/
Vocabulary: Following Oral Directions
Fine Motor Skills: Tracing

Unit 9   Letter J 54
Phonemic Awareness: Listening for the /j/ Sound
Vocabulary: Following Oral Directions
Comprehension: Categorizing
Visual Discrimination: Seeing the Whole; Identifying Missing Parts
Fine Motor Skills: Using Scissors; Tracing; Drawing

Unit 10   Letter V 60
Phonemic Awareness: Listening for the /v/ Sound
Vocabulary: Following Oral Directions
Comprehension: Sequencing
Visual Discrimination: Seeing the Whole; Identifying Likenesses and Differences
Fine Motor Skills: Using Scissors; Tracing

Unit 11   Letter K 66
Phonemic Awareness: Listening for the /k/ Sound
Vocabulary: Following Oral Directions
Visual Discrimination: Seeing the Whole; Identifying Likenesses and Differences; Identifying Missing Parts
Fine Motor Skills: Using Scissors; Tracing; Drawing; Tracking Left to Right

Unit 12   Letter D 72
Phonemic Awareness: Listening for the /d/ Sound
Vocabulary: Following Oral Directions
Comprehension: Predicting
Visual Discrimination: Seeing the Whole;
Identifying Likenesses and Differences
Fine Motor Skills: Using Scissors; Tracing

Review J, V, K, D 78
Phonemic Awareness: Listening for the Sounds
of /j/, /v/, /k/, /d/
Vocabulary: Following Oral Directions
Fine Motor Skills: Tracing

Unit 13   Letter N 80
Phonemic Awareness: Listening for the /n/ Sound
Vocabulary: Following Oral Directions
Comprehension: Sequencing
Visual Discrimination: Seeing the Whole;
Identifying Likenesses and Differences
Fine Motor Skills: Using Scissors; Tracing

Unit 14   Letter P 84
Phonemic Awareness: Listening for the /p/ Sound
Vocabulary: Following Oral Directions
Comprehension: Predicting; Categorizing
Visual Discrimination: Seeing the Whole;
Identifying Likenesses and Differences
Fine Motor Skills: Using Scissors; Tracing

Unit 15   Letter Y 90
Phonemic Awareness: Listening for the /y/ Sound;
Listening for Rhyming Words
Vocabulary: Following Oral Directions
Comprehension: Predicting; Sequencing
Visual Discrimination: Seeing the Whole
Fine Motor Skills: Using Scissors; Tracing

Unit 16   Letter S 96
Phonemic Awareness: Listening for the /s/ Sound;
Rhyming
Vocabulary: Following Oral Directions
Visual Discrimination: Seeing the Whole;
Identifying Likenesses and Differences; Finding
Like Objects
Fine Motor Skills: Using Scissors; Tracing

Review N, P, Y, S 102
Phonemic Awareness: Listening for the
Sounds of /n/, /p/, /y/, /s/
Vocabulary: Following Oral Directions
Fine Motor Skills: Tracing

Unit 17   Letter T 104
Phonemic Awareness: Listening for the /t/ Sound
Vocabulary: Following Oral Directions
Comprehension: Sequencing; Categorizing
Visual Discrimination: Seeing the Whole
Fine Motor Skills: Using Scissors; Tracing

Unit 18   Letter W 110
Phonemic Awareness: Listening for the /w/ Sound
Vocabulary: Following Oral Directions
Comprehension: Predicting
Visual Discrimination: Seeing the Whole;
Identifying Likenesses and Differences; Identifying
Missing Parts
Fine Motor Skills: Using Scissors; Drawing;
Tracing

Unit 19   Letter Z 116
Phonemic Awareness: Listening for the /z/ Sound
Vocabulary: Following Oral Directions
Comprehension: Predicting; Categorizing
Visual Discrimination: Seeing the Whole;
Recognizing Objects by Shape
Fine Motor Skills: Using Scissors; Tracing

Unit 20   Letters QU 122
Phonemic Awareness: Listening for the /qu/
Sound; Listening for Rhyming Words
Vocabulary: Following Oral Directions
Comprehension: Predicting
Visual Discrimination: Seeing the Whole; Tracing

Unit 21   Letter X 126
Phonemic Awareness: Listening for the Ending
Sound of /x/; Listening for Rhyming Words
Vocabulary: Following Oral Directions
Visual Discrimination: Seeing the Whole;
Identifying Likenesses and Differences; Identifying
Missing Parts
Fine Motor Skills: Tracing; Drawing

Review T, W, Z, QU, X 130
Phonemic Awareness: Listening for the
Sounds of /t/, /w/, /z/, /qu/, and Ending Sound
of /x /
Vocabulary: Following Oral Directions
Fine Motor Skills: Tracing

Tracking Form 132

Answer Key 134

Dear Parents or Guardians,

The activities in this book are designed to help children acquire early literacy skills and prepare them for the exciting world of reading! This book introduces each consonant and contains tasks that reinforce the letter-sound each consonant makes.

Because letters that are similar in shape or sound can be confusing for emergent readers, consonants have been introduced in a strategic way.

Provide any help your child may need to complete the activity pages.

- Read the directions to your child.
- Answer any questions your child has about how to complete the activity.
- Encourage your child to complete predictable pages independently.
- Help your child check completed work.

There are many ways you can build your child's early literacy skills and help prepare your child to become a successful reader.

- After a letter is introduced, have your child look for it. Point out signs or trademarks that your child sees every day. Emergent readers learn by reading the familiar words around them.

- Play with the sounds of language—make up silly words, create rhymes, and sing funny songs with your child. Books, songs, rhymes, and language games are the foundation on which phonemic awareness is built.

- Read to your child. Set aside a particular time of the day for reading a book together. Read the signs at parks, stores, playgrounds, and museums. Build your child's at-home library, or make frequent visits to the public library.

- Reinforce language by talking with your child and listening to what your child has to say.

- Be a reader yourself. Read books, magazines, and newspapers. Read signs, labels, letters, and directions. Your child will want to read because your example says "reading is important." The desire to read is a key component to achieving reading success.

Sincerely,
Evan-Moor

Listen for the Sound

B b

See the bat.

They all start like **bat**.

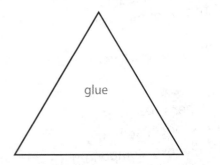  

Parents: Name the pictures with your child. (ball, box, bee)

Cut.

Glue.

Cut out the pieces.
Glue them to page 4.

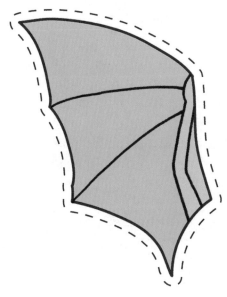

Name the pictures.
Cut out the shapes.
Glue them to page 4.

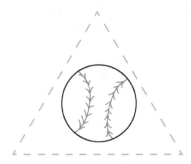

Fly Away Home

Trace the bat's path to his cave.

Trace the letters.

B B B B b b b b

Day and Night

Draw lines to match.

It Rhymes with Bat

Color the pictures that rhyme with **bat**.

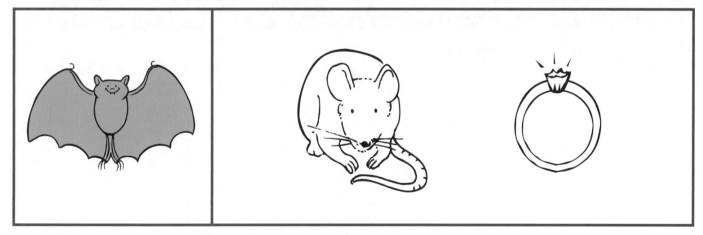

Listen for the Sound

See the rabbit.

They all start like **rabbit**.

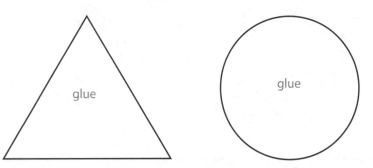

Parents: Name the pictures with your child. (rose, rake, ring)

Cut.

Glue.

Cut out the pieces.
Glue them to page 10.

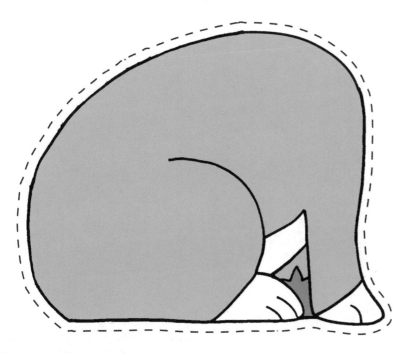

Name the pictures.
Cut out the shapes.
Glue them to page 10.

R Is for Rabbit

Trace the rabbit.
Color the rabbit brown.

Trace the letters.

Hungry Rabbit

This is a rabbit.

This is what the rabbit sees.

Circle what the rabbit will do.

Shadows

Draw a line.
Match each picture with its shadow.

Listen for the Sound

See the fish.

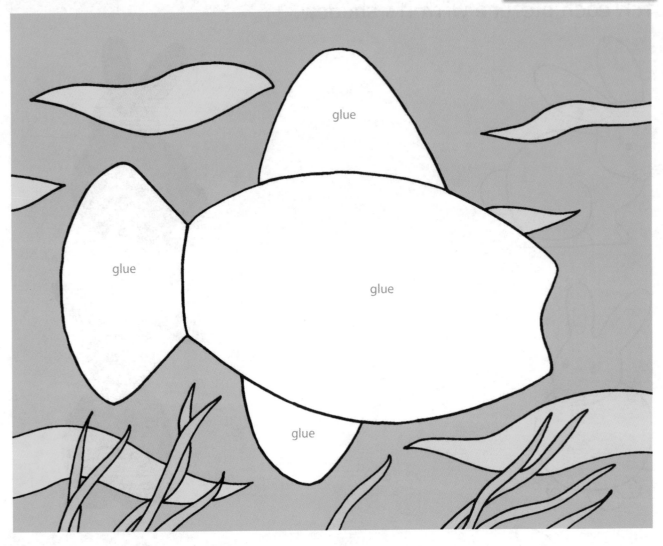

They all start like **fish**.

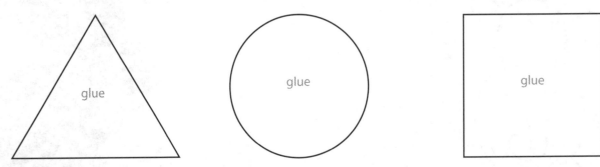

Parents: Name the pictures with your child. (four, fox, feather)

Cut.

Glue.

Cut out the pieces.
Glue them to page 16.

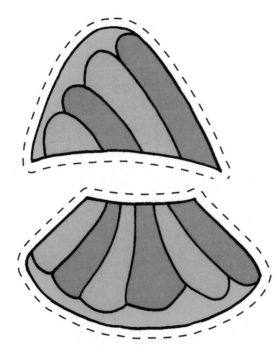

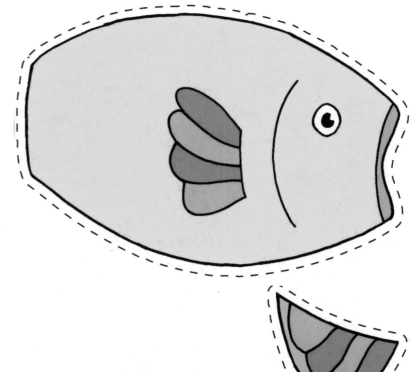

Name the pictures.
Cut out the shapes.
Glue them to page 16.

Animal Hunt

A fish is an animal.
Circle the animals.

Same or Different?

Circle the fish in each row that are the same.

Funny Fish

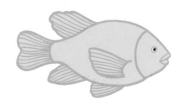

Color the pictures that begin like **fish**.

Trace the letters.

Listen for the Sound

Cc

See the cat.

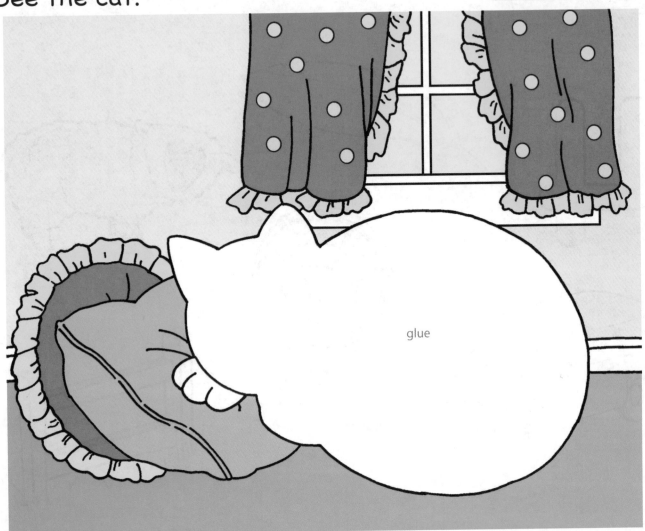

They all start like cat.

Parents: Name the pictures with your child. (car, cake, cup)

Cut.

Glue.

Cut out the pieces.
Glue them to page 22.

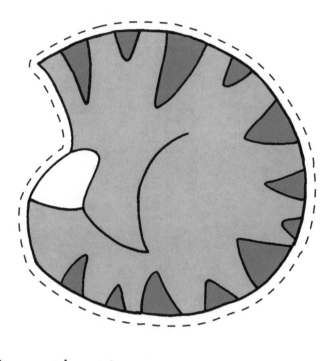

Name the pictures.
Cut out the shapes.
Glue them to page 22.

The Hungry Cat

Cut out the pictures.
Glue them in order.
Color.

1 | glue

2 | glue

3 | glue

Finish the Cats

Draw what
is missing.

Color to match.

Cat Fun

Connect the dots.

Trace the letters.

Do They Start the Same?

Color 😊 or ☹.
    yes   no

Trace and Match

Trace the letters.
Draw a line to make a match.

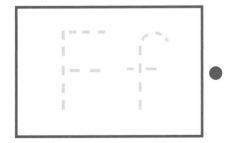 

Listen for the Sound

See the monkey.

They all start like **monkey**.

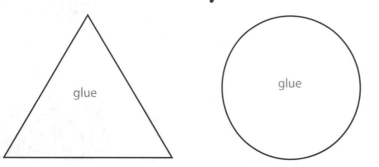

Parents: Name the pictures with your child. (mouse, milk, moon)

Cut.

Glue.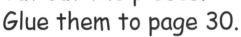

Cut out the pieces.
Glue them to page 30.

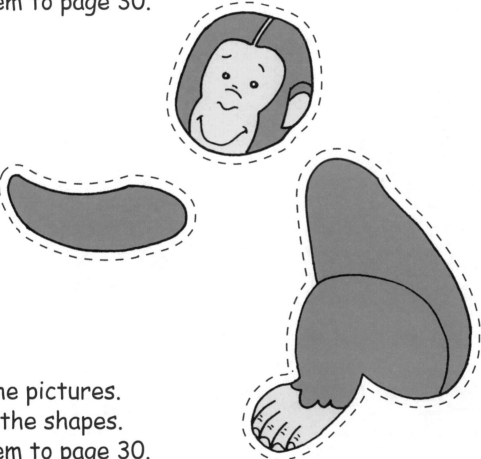

Name the pictures.
Cut out the shapes.
Glue them to page 30.

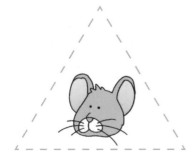

What Will Happen?

This is a monkey.

This is what the monkey sees.

Circle what the monkey will do.

Finish the Monkey

Look at the monkey.   Draw what is missing.

Trace the letters.

Grab the Bananas

Start at the  .

Trace the line to the .

Listen for the Sound

See the lamb.

They all start like **lamb**.

Parents: Name the pictures with your child. (lamp, lock, lion)

Skill Sharpeners—Reading • EMC 4527 • © Evan-Moor Corp.

Cut.

Glue.

Cut out the pieces.
Glue them to page 36.

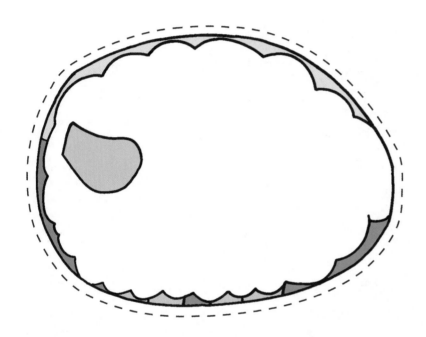

Name the pictures.
Cut out the shapes.
Glue them to page 36.

Back to the Barn

Trace the line.
Help the lamb back to the barn.

Same or Different?

Circle the pictures in each row that are the same.

Trace the letters.

Skill Sharpeners—Reading • EMC 4527 • © Evan-Moor Corp.

Find the Lambs

Color the lambs.

Are there 3 in a row? yes no

Listen for the Sound

Gg

Trace the horns.
Color the goat.

See the goat.

They all start like **goat**.

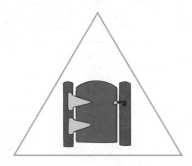  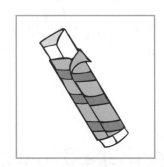

Parents: Name the pictures with your child. (gate, girl, gum)

Goat

Trace.

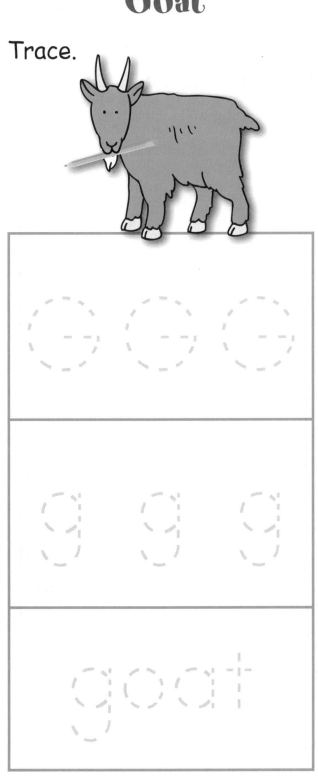

Little Goat Grows Up

Cut out the pictures.
Glue them in order.

1

glue

2

glue

3

glue

It Rhymes with Goat

Color the pictures that rhyme with **goat**.

Listen for the Sound

Hh

See the hen.

They all start like **hen**.

Parents: Name the pictures with your child. (hat, heart, hand)

Skill Sharpeners—Reading • EMC 4527 • © Evan-Moor Corp.

Cut.

Glue.

Cut out the pieces.
Glue them to page 46.

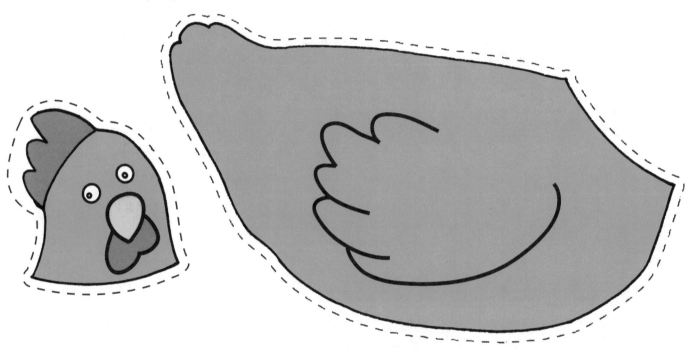

Name the pictures.
Cut out the shapes.
Glue them to page 46.

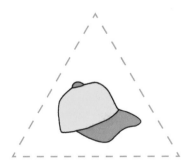

What Will Happen?

This is a mother hen.

This is the hen's nest.

Circle what the hen will do.

Same or Different?

Circle the pictures in each row that are the same.

Trace the letters.

Birds

A hen is a bird.
Circle all the birds.
Color them.

Do They Start the Same?

Color 😊 or 🙁 .
yes   no

yes   no

yes   no

yes   no

yes   no

Trace and Match

Trace the letters.
Draw a line to make a match.

 •

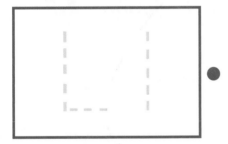 •

 •

 •

J j

Listen for the Sound

See the jet.

glue

They all start like **jet**.

glue

glue

glue

Parents: Name the pictures with your child. (jeep, jacket, jar)

Cut.

Glue.

Cut out the pieces.
Glue them to page 54.

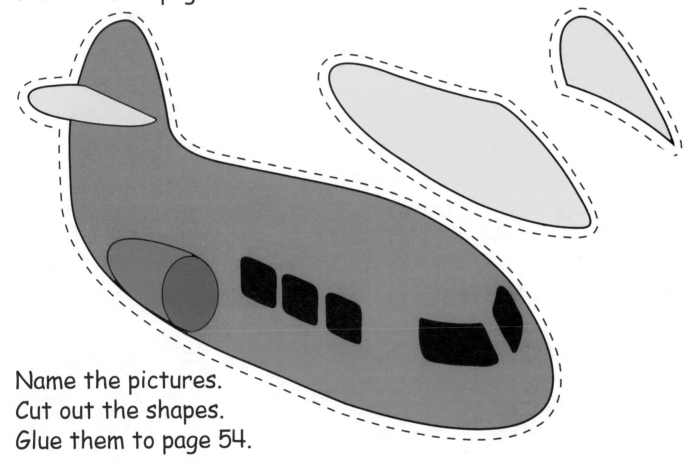

Name the pictures.
Cut out the shapes.
Glue them to page 54.

Jet

Trace the path of the jet.

Fly Away

A jet can fly.
Color the pictures of other things that can fly.

Finish the Jet

Draw what is missing.
Color the jet to match.

Trace the letters.

Listen for the Sound

V v

See the vulture.

They all start like **vulture**.

Parents: Name the pictures with your child. (violin, vest, vase)

Skill Sharpeners—Reading • EMC 4527 • © Evan-Moor Corp.

Cut.

Glue.

Cut out the pieces.
Glue them to page 60.

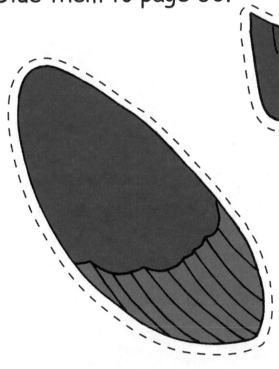

Name the pictures.
Cut out the shapes.
Glue them to page 60.

V Is for Vulture

Trace the wing.
Color the vulture.

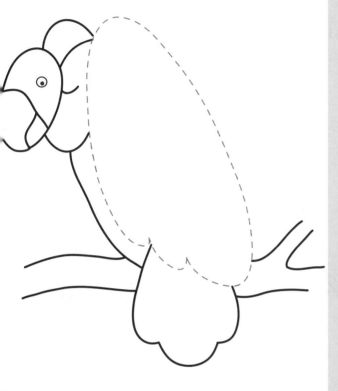

Trace the letters.

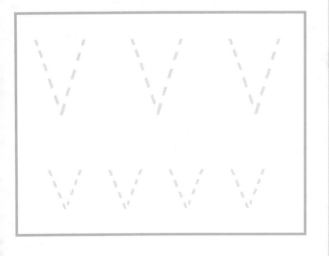

Vulture Grows Up

Cut out the pictures.
Glue them in order.

1

glue

2

glue

3

glue

Same or Different?

Circle the pictures in each row that are the same.

Listen for the Sound

Kk

See the kangaroo.

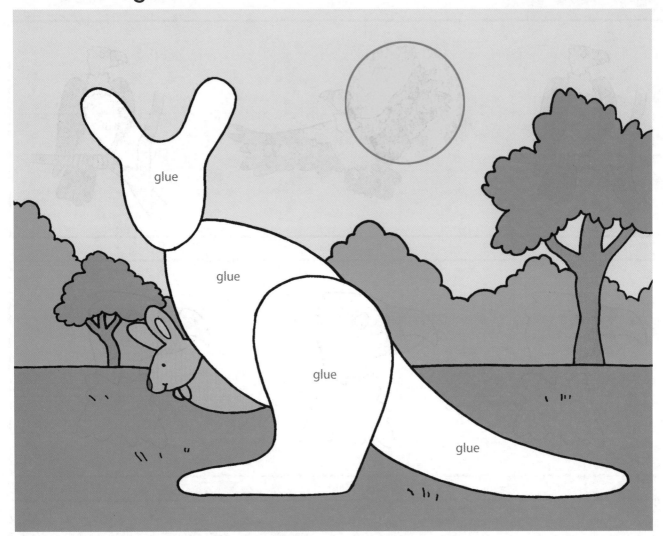

They all start like **kangaroo**.

Parents: Name the pictures with your child. (kite, kitten, key)

Cut.

Glue.

Cut out the pieces.
Glue them to page 66.

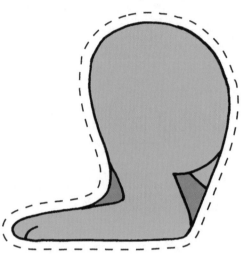

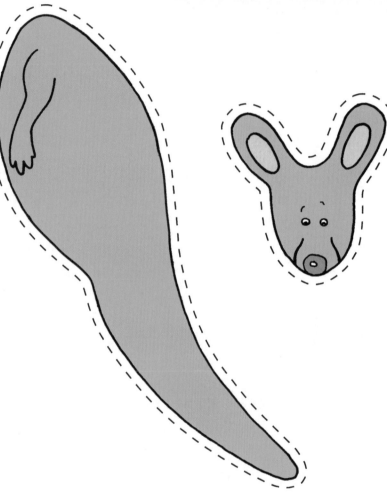

Name the pictures.
Cut out the shapes.
Glue them to page 66.

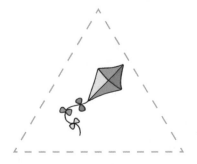

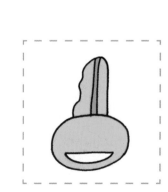

Kangaroos Hop

Trace.

Trace the letters.

Kangaroo Fun

Circle the kangaroos that are the same.

Finish the Kangaroo

Color the kangaroos.

Draw what is missing.

Dd

Listen for the Sound

See the duck.

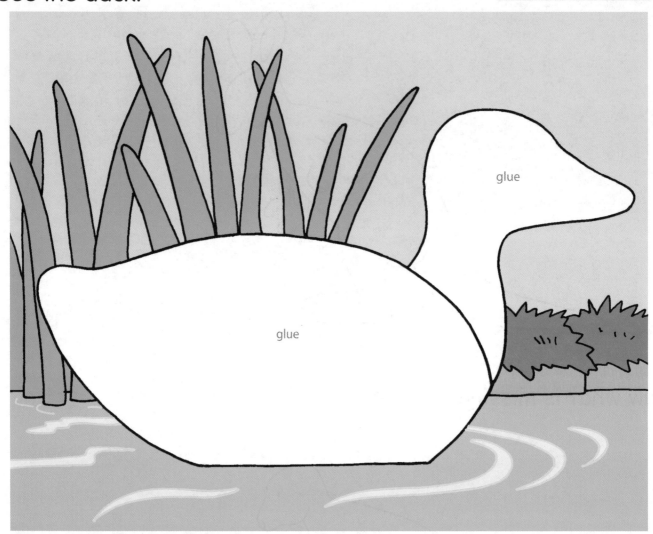

They all start like **duck**.

Parents: Name the pictures with your child. (door, desk, dog)

Cut.

Glue.

Cut out the pieces.
Glue them to page 72.

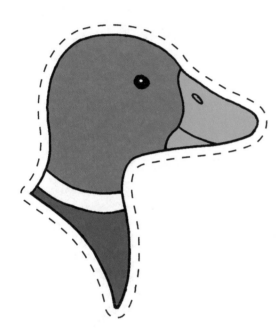

Name the pictures.
Cut out the shapes.
Glue them to page 72.

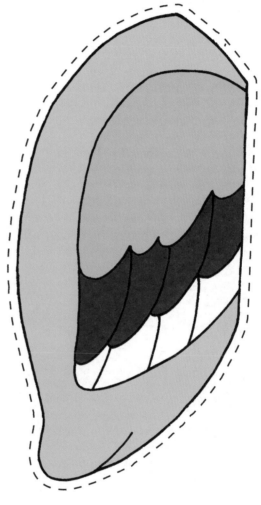

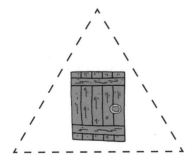

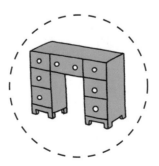

What Will Happen?

This is a duck.

Look what the duck sees.

Circle what the duck will do.

D Is for Duck

Trace the duck.
Color the duck.

Trace the letters.

Skill Sharpeners—Reading • EMC 4527 • © Evan-Moor Corp.

Make a Match

Circle the pictures in each row that are the same.

Do They Start the Same?

Color or .

yes　　　no

yes　　no

yes　　no

yes　　no

yes　　no

Trace and Match

Trace the letters.
Draw a line to make a match.

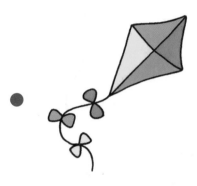

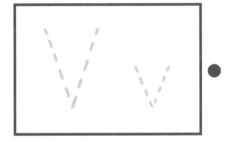

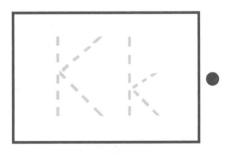

Listen for the Sound

Trace the nest.
Color.

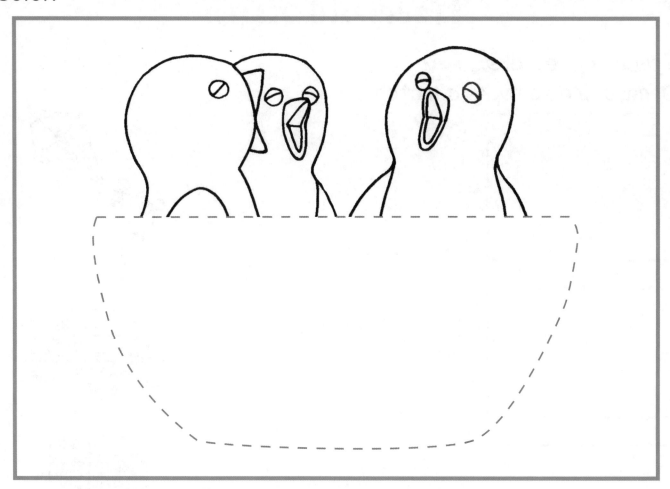

They all start like **nest**.

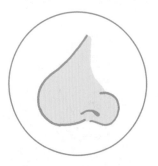

Parents: Name the pictures with your child. (nickel, nose, net)

Fly Home

Trace.

Build a Nest

Cut out the pictures.
Glue them in order.

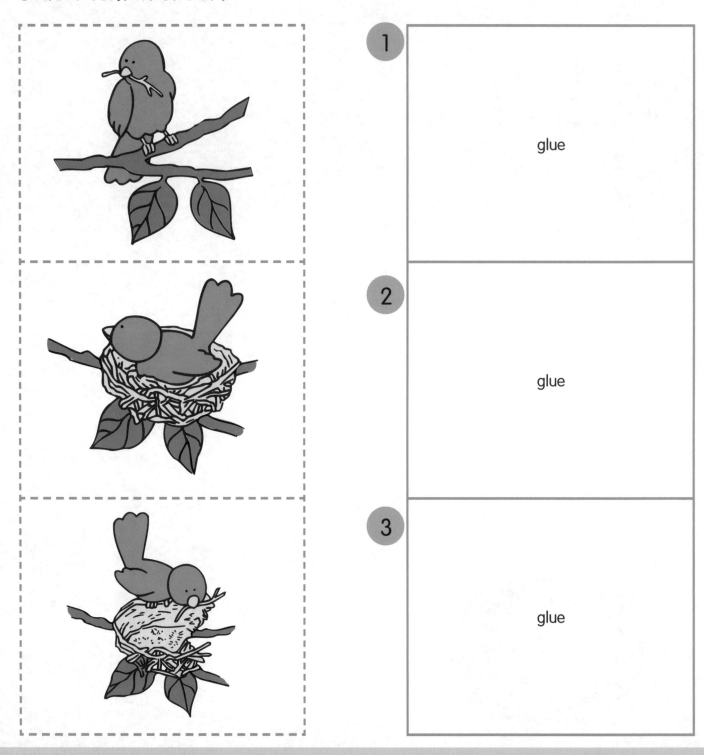

1

glue

2

glue

3

glue

Same or Different?

Circle the pictures in each row that are the same.

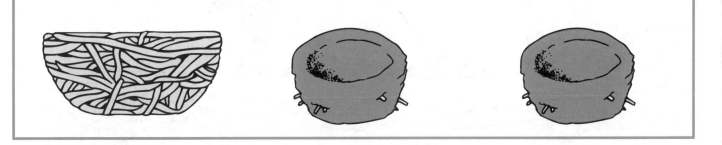

Trace the letters.

Listen for the Sound

P p

See the penguin.

They all start like **penguin**.

Parents: Name the pictures with your child. (pear, pumpkin, pig)

Skill Sharpeners—Reading • EMC 4527 • © Evan-Moor Corp.

Cut.

Glue.

Cut out the pieces.
Glue them to page 84.

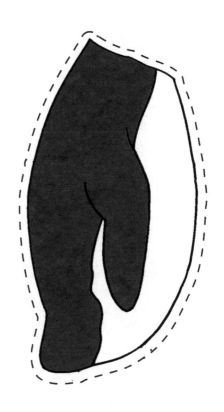

Name the pictures.
Cut out the shapes.
Glue them to page 84.

What Will Happen?

This is a penguin.

Look what the penguin sees.

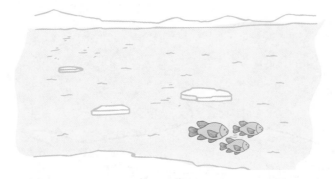

Circle what the penguin will do.

Swimming

A penguin can swim.
Color the pictures of other things that can swim.

Same or Different?

Circle the pictures in each row that are the same.

Trace the letters.

Listen for the Sound

See the yarn.

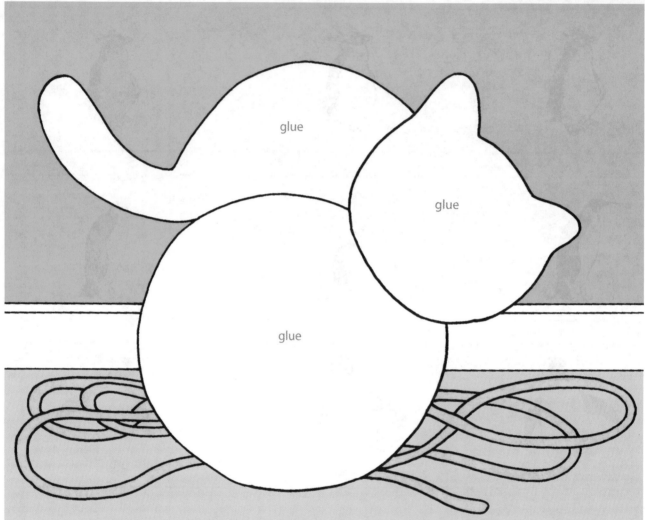

They all start like **yarn.**

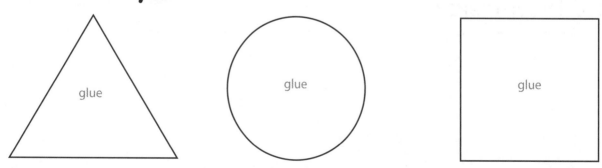

Parents: Name the pictures with your child. (yak, yo-yo, yellow)

Cut.

Glue.

Cut out the pieces.
Glue them to page 90.

Name the pictures.
Cut out the shapes.
Glue them to page 90.

What Will It Be?

Trace to make a match.

A Surprise for Puppy

Cut out the pictures.
Glue them in order.

1

glue

2

glue

3

glue

Find the Rhyme

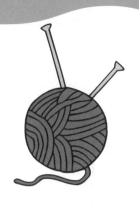

Connect the dots to complete the picture that rhymes with **yarn**.

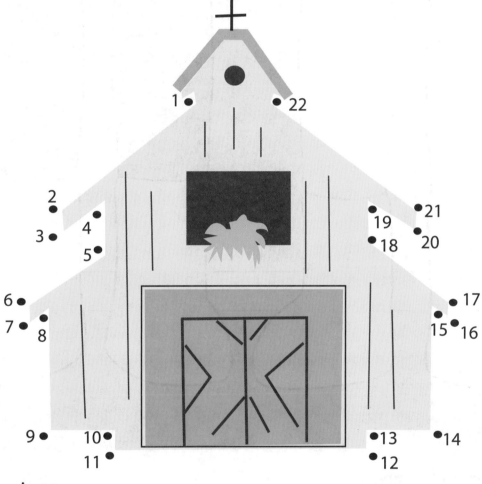

1
22
2
3
4
5
21
19
18
20
6
7
8
17
15
16
9
10
11
13
14
12

Trace the letters.

Y Y Y Y Y Y Y Y

Trace the letters.

Listen for the Sound

S s

See the socks.

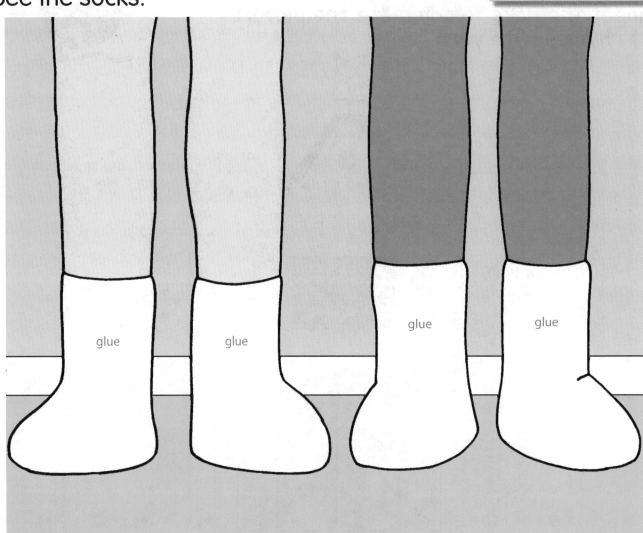

They all start like **socks**.

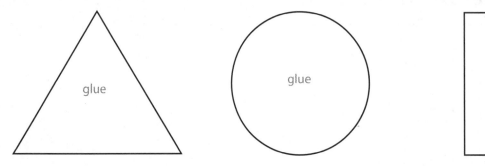

Parents: Name the pictures with your child. (soap, six, sun)

Cut.

Glue.

Cut out the pieces.
Glue them to page 96.

Name the pictures.
Cut out the shapes.
Glue them to page 96.

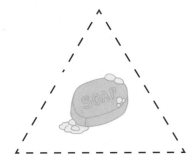

Find My Socks

Color the socks hiding in the picture.

How many socks did you find?

Make Pairs of Socks

Draw to make the socks look the same.

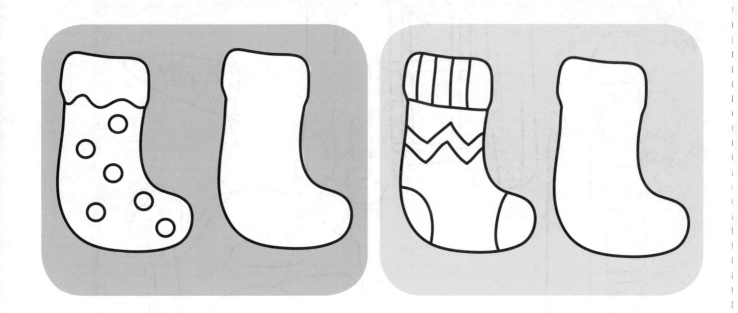

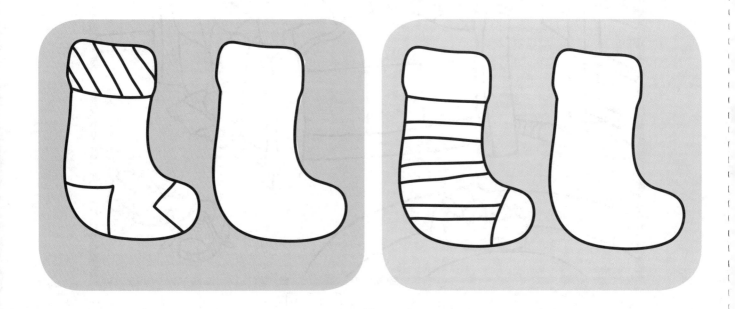

Skill Sharpeners—Reading • EMC 4527 • © Evan-Moor Corp.

It Rhymes with Sock

Color the pictures that rhyme with **sock**.

Trace the letters.

Do They Start the Same?

Color 😊 or 😞 .
yes   no

Trace and Match

Trace the letters.
Draw a line to make a match.

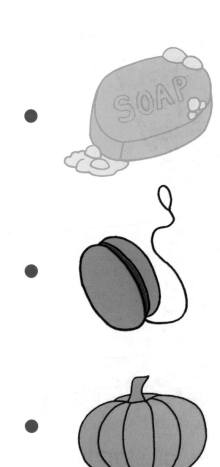

T t

Listen for the Sound

See the tent.

They all start like **tent**.

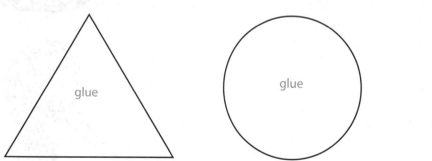

Parents: Name the pictures with your child. (teeth, ten, turtle)

Cut.

Glue.

Cut out the pieces.
Glue them to page 104.

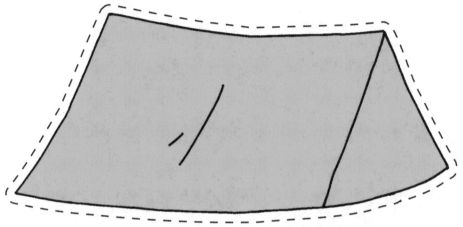
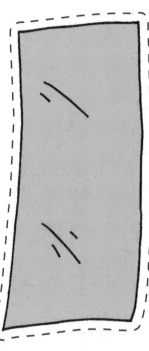
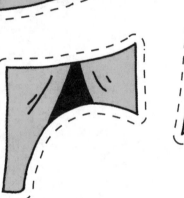

Name the pictures.
Cut out the shapes.
Glue them to page 104.

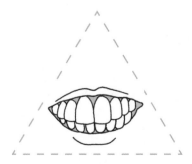

T Is for Tent

Color the tent.

Trace the letters.

A Tent

Cut out the pictures.
Glue them in order.

1
| |
|glue|

2
| |
|glue|

3
| |
|glue|

Camping

Color the pictures of things for camping.

Listen for the Sound

W w

See the wagon.

They all start like **wagon**.

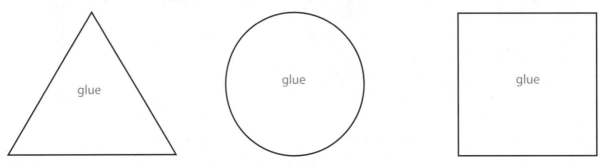

Parents: Name the pictures with your child. (wolf, watch, window)

Cut.

Glue.

Cut out the pieces.
Glue them to page 110.

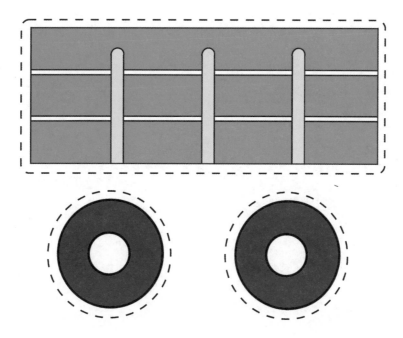

Name the pictures.
Cut out the shapes.
Glue them to page 110.

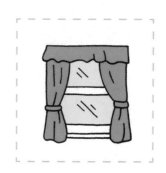

Same or Different?

Circle the pictures in each row that are the same.

What Will Happen?

Look at the boy.
See what he has.

Circle what the boy will do.

Skill Sharpeners—Reading • EMC 4527 • © Evan-Moor Corp.

Finish the Wagon

Draw what is missing.
Color it to match.

Trace the letters.

Listen for the Sound

Zz

See the zebra.

glue

They all start like **zebra**.

glue

glue

glue

Parents: Name the pictures with your child. (zigzag, zero, zipper)

Cut.

Glue.

Cut out the pieces.
Glue them to page 116.

Name the pictures.
Cut out the shapes.
Glue them to page 116.

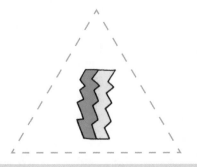

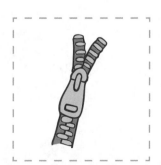

Shadows

Draw lines to make a match.

What Will Happen?

This is a zebra.

This is what the zebra sees.

Circle what the zebra will do.

Black and White

A zebra is black and white.
Draw another black and white animal.

Trace the letters.

Z Z Z Z Z Z Z

Queen

Trace the crown.
Color the queen.

They all start like **queen**.

Parents: Name the pictures with your child. (quilt, quail, quarter)

What Will Happen?

This is the queen.

Look what the queen sees.

Circle what the queen will do.

To the Castle

Help the queen find the castle.

Skill Sharpeners—Reading • EMC 4527 • © Evan-Moor Corp.

Rhyme Time

Draw a line to match the pictures that rhyme.

red

green

brown

Trace the letters.

Listen for the Sound

Trace the fox.
Color it.

fo<u>x</u>

They all end like **fox**.

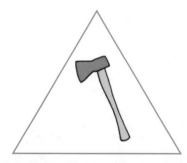

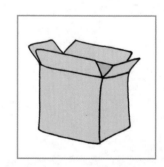

Parents: Name the pictures with your child. (ax, six, box)

It Rhymes with Fox

Color the pictures that rhyme with **fox**.

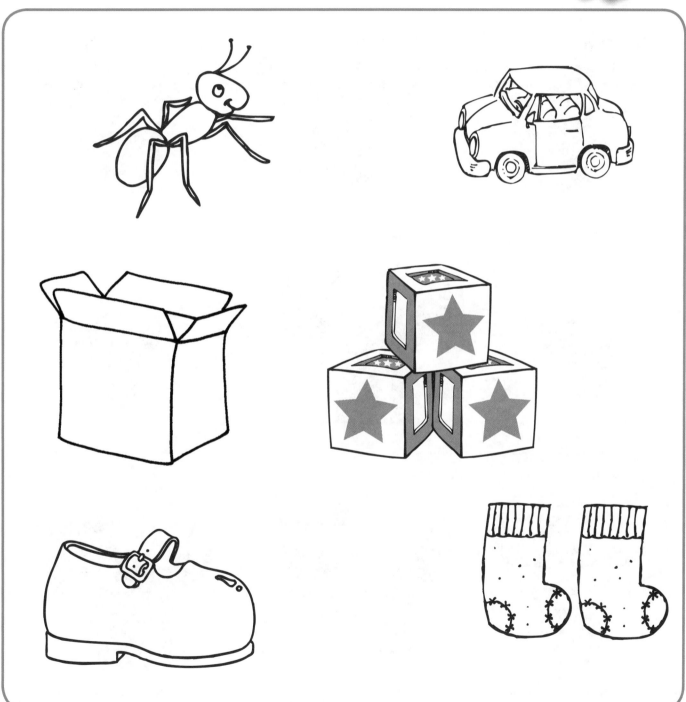

Same or Different?

Circle the pictures in each row that are the same.

Finish the Fox

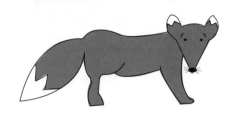

Draw what is missing.
Color to match.

Trace the letters.

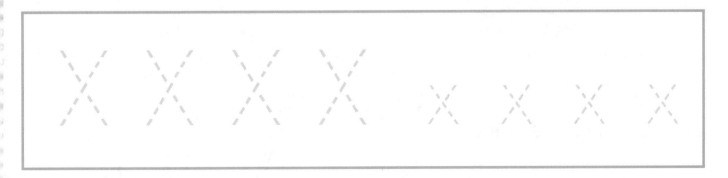

Do They Start the Same?

Color 😊 or ☹ .
yes   no

yes   no

yes   no

yes   no

yes   no

Do they end the same?

yes   no

Trace and Match

Trace the letters.
Draw a line to make a match.

 •   •

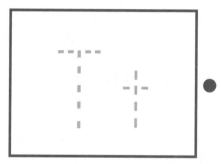 •   •

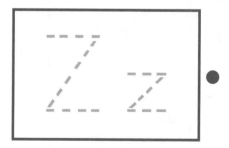 •   •

 •   •

Tracking Form

Topic	Color in each page you complete.					
Unit 1 Letter B	4	5	6	7	8	9
Unit 2 Letter R	10	11	12	13	14	15
Unit 3 Letter F	16	17	18	19	20	21
Unit 4 Letter C	22	23	24	25	26	27
Review B, R, F, C	28	29				
Unit 5 Letter M	30	31	32	33	34	35
Unit 6 Letter L	36	37	38	39	40	41
Unit 7 Letter G	42	43	44	45		
Unit 8 Letter H	46	47	48	49	50	51
Review M, L, G, H	52	53				
Unit 9 Letter J	54	55	56	57	58	59
Unit 10 Letter V	60	61	62	63	64	65
Unit 11 Letter K	66	67	68	69	70	71
Unit 12 Letter D	72	73	74	75	76	77
Review J, V, K, D	78	79				
Unit 13 Letter N	80	81	82	83		
Unit 14 Letter P	84	85	86	87	88	89
Unit 15 Letter Y	90	91	92	93	94	95
Unit 16 Letter S	96	97	98	99	100	101
Review N, P, Y, S	102	103				

Tracking Form

Topic	Color in each page you complete.					
Unit 17 Letter T	104	105	106	107	108	109
Unit 18 Letter W	110	111	112	113	114	115
Unit 19 Letter Z	116	117	118	119	120	121
Unit 20 Letters QU	122	123	124	125		
Unit 21 Letter X	126	127	128	129		
Review T, W, Z, QU, X	130	131				

Answer Key

Page 4

Page 7

Page 8

Page 9

Page 10

Page 13

Page 14

Page 15

Page 16

Page 19

Animal Hunt

A fish is an animal.
Circle the animals.

Page 20

Same or Different?

Circle the fish in each row that are the same.

Page 21

Funny Fish

Color the pictures that begin like **fish**.

Trace the letters.

F F F F f f f f

Page 22

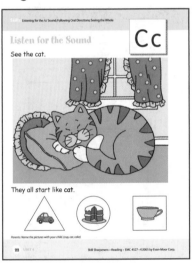

Listen for the Sound

Cc

See the cat.

They all start like **cat**.

Page 25

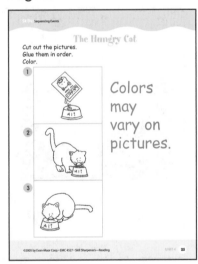

The Hungry Cat

Cut out the pictures.
Glue them in order.
Color.

Colors may vary on pictures.

Page 26

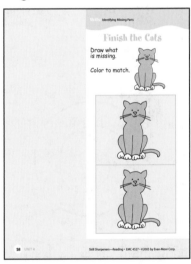

Finish the Cats

Draw what is missing.

Color to match.

Page 27

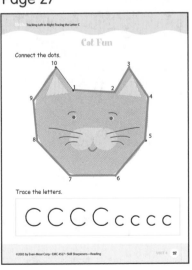

Cat Fun

Connect the dots.

Trace the letters.

C C C C c c c c

Page 28

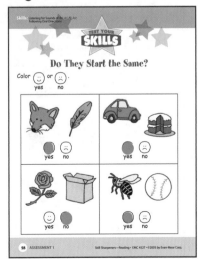

Do They Start the Same?

Color 😊 or ☹
yes no

Page 29

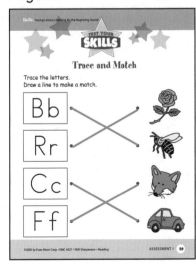

Trace and Match

Trace the letters.
Draw a line to make a match.

Bb
Rr
Cc
Ff

Page 30

Listen for the Sound

Mm

See the monkey.

They all start like **monkey**.

Parents: Name the pictures with your child. (moon, mouse, milk)

30 UNIT 5   Skill Sharpeners—Reading • EMC 4527 • ©2005 by Evan-Moor Corp.

Page 33

What Will Happen?

This is a monkey.

This is what the monkey sees.

Circle what the monkey will do.

©2005 by Evan-Moor Corp. • EMC 4527 • Skill Sharpeners—Reading   UNIT 5 33

Page 34

Finish the Monkey

Look at the monkey.   Draw what is missing.

Trace the letters.

M M M m m m

34 UNIT 5   Skill Sharpeners—Reading • EMC 4527 • ©2005 by Evan-Moor Corp.

Page 35

Grab the Bananas

Start at the

Trace the line to the

©2005 by Evan-Moor Corp. • EMC 4527 • Skill Sharpeners—Reading   UNIT 5 35

Page 36

Listen for the Sound

Ll

See the lamb.

They all start like **lamb**.

Parents: Name the pictures with your child. (lion, lamp, lock)

36 UNIT 6   Skill Sharpeners—Reading • EMC 4527 • ©2005 by Evan-Moor Corp.

Page 39

Back to the Barn

Trace the line.
Help the lamb back to the barn.

©2005 by Evan-Moor Corp. • EMC 4527 • Skill Sharpeners—Reading   UNIT 6 39

Page 40

Same or Different?

Circle the pictures in each row that are the same.

Trace the letters.

L L L L l l l l

40 UNIT 6   Skill Sharpeners—Reading • EMC 4527 • ©2005 by Evan-Moor Corp.

Page 41

Find the Lambs

Color the lambs.   Colors will vary.

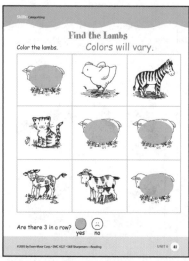

Are there 3 in a row?   yes   no

©2005 by Evan-Moor Corp. • EMC 4527 • Skill Sharpeners—Reading   UNIT 6 41

Page 42

Listen for the Sound

Gg

Trace the horns.
Color the goat.

Colors may vary.

See the goat.

They all start like **goat**.

Parents: Name the pictures with your child. (gate, girl, gum)

42 UNIT 7   Skill Sharpeners—Reading • EMC 4527 • ©2005 by Evan-Moor Corp.

Page 43

Page 44

Page 45

Page 46

Page 49

Page 50

Page 51

Page 52

Page 53

Page 54

Page 57

Page 58

Page 59

Page 60

Page 63

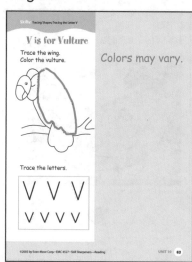

Page 64

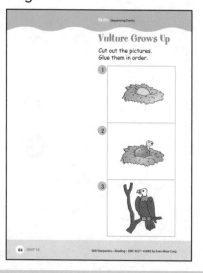

Page 65

Page 66

Page 69

Page 70

Page 71

Page 72

Page 75

Page 76

Page 77

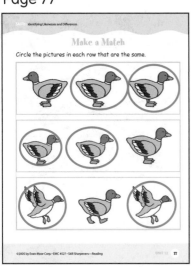

Page 78

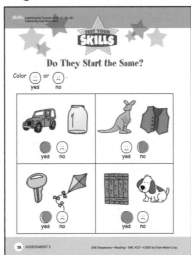

Page 79

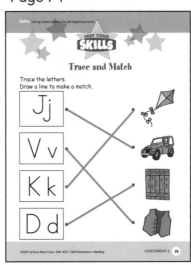

Page 80

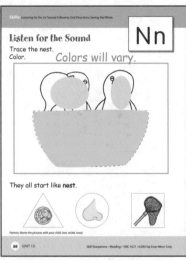

Skills: Listening for the /n/ Sound; Following Oral Directions; Seeing the Whole

Listen for the Sound

Nn

Trace the nest.
Color. Colors will vary.

They all start like **nest**.

Parents: Name the pictures with your child. (net, nickel, nose)

80 UNIT 13   Skill Sharpeners—Reading • EMC 4527 • ©2005 by Evan-Moor Corp.

Page 81

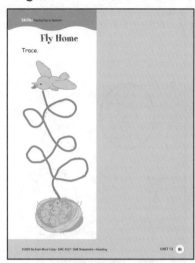

Skills: Tracing Top to Bottom

Fly Home

Trace.

©2005 by Evan-Moor Corp. • EMC 4527 • Skill Sharpeners—Reading   UNIT 13 81

Page 82

Skills: Sequencing Events

Build a Nest

Cut out the pictures.
Glue them in order.

1
2
3

83 UNIT 13   Skill Sharpeners—Reading • EMC 4527 • ©2005 by Evan-Moor Corp.

Page 83

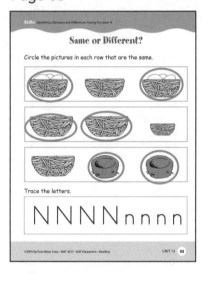

Skills: Identifying Likenesses and Differences; Tracing the Letter N

Same or Different?

Circle the pictures in each row that are the same.

Trace the letters.

N N N N n n n n

©2005 by Evan-Moor Corp. • EMC 4527 • Skill Sharpeners—Reading   UNIT 13 83

Page 84

Skills: Listening for the /p/ Sound; Following Oral Directions; Seeing the Whole

Listen for the Sound

Pp

See the penguin.

They all start like **penguin**.

Parents: Name the pictures with your child. (pear, pig, pumpkin)

84 UNIT 14   Skill Sharpeners—Reading • EMC 4527 • ©2005 by Evan-Moor Corp.

Page 87

Skills: Predicting What Will Happen Next

What Will Happen?

This is a penguin.

Look what the penguin sees.

Circle what the penguin will do.

©2005 by Evan-Moor Corp. • EMC 4527 • Skill Sharpeners—Reading   UNIT 14 87

Page 88

Skills: Categorizing

Swimming

A penguin can swim.
Color the pictures of other things that can swim.

88 UNIT 14   Skill Sharpeners—Reading • EMC 4527 • ©2005 by Evan-Moor Corp.

Page 89

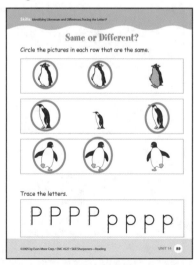

Skills: Identifying Likenesses and Differences; Tracing the Letter P

Same or Different?

Circle the pictures in each row that are the same.

Trace the letters.

P P P P p p p p

©2005 by Evan-Moor Corp. • EMC 4527 • Skill Sharpeners—Reading   UNIT 14 89

Page 90

Skills: Listening for the /y/ Sound; Following Oral Directions; Seeing the Whole

Listen for the Sound

Yy

See the yarn.

They all start like **yarn**.

Parents: Name the pictures with your child. (yellow, yak, yo-yo)

90 UNIT 15   Skill Sharpeners—Reading • EMC 4527 • ©2005 by Evan-Moor Corp.

Page 93

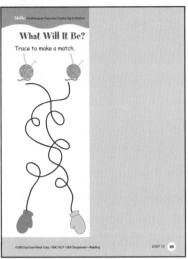

Page 94

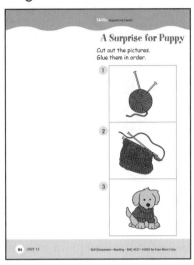

Page 95

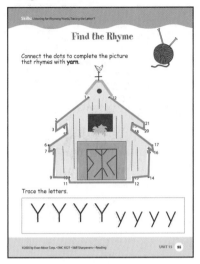

Page 96

Page 99

Page 100

Page 101

Page 102

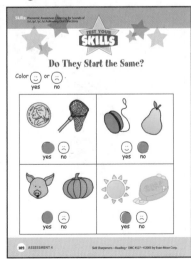

Page 103

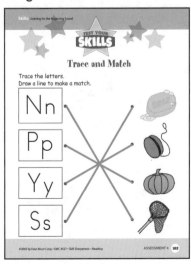

Page 104

Page 107

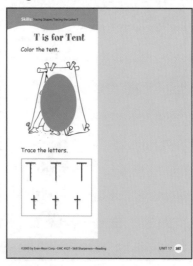

Page 108

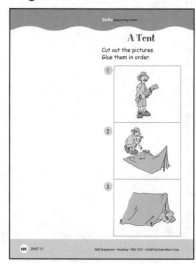

Page 109

Page 110

Page 113

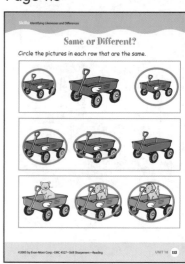

Page 114

Page 115

Page 116

Page 119

Page 120

Page 121

Page 122

Page 123

Page 124

Page 125

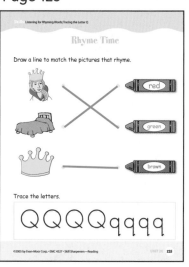

Page 126

Page 127

Page 128

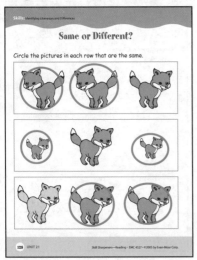

Page 129

Page 130

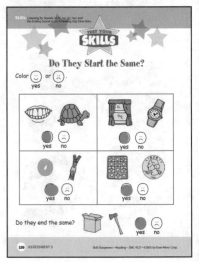

Page 131

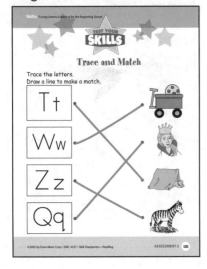